W9-BBO-740

Put Beginning Readers on the Right Track with ALL ABOARD READING™

The All Aboard Reading series is especially for beginning readers. Written by noted authors and illustrated in full color, these are books that children really and truly *want* to read—books to excite their imagination, tickle their funny bone, expand their interests, and support their feelings. With four different reading levels, All Aboard Reading lets you choose which books are most appropriate for your children and their growing abilities.

Picture Readers—for Ages 3 to 6
Picture Readers have super-simple texts, with many nouns appearing as rebus pictures. At the end of each book are 24 flash cards—on one side is the rebus picture; on the other side is the written-out word.

Level 1—for Preschool through First-Grade Children
Level 1 books have very few lines per page, very large type, easy words, lots of repetition, and pictures with visual "cues" to help children figure out the words on the page.

Level 2—for First-Grade to Third-Grade Children
Level 2 books are printed in slightly smaller type than Level 1 books. The stories are more complex, but there is still lots of repetition in the text, and many pictures. The sentences are quite simple and are broken up into short lines to make reading easier.

Level 3—for Second-Grade through Third-Grade Children
Level 3 books have considerably longer texts, harder words, and more complicated sentences.

All Aboard for happy reading!

Dedicated in memory of Dale Earnhardt—A.G.

For Adam—J.S.

Photo credits: p. 5, Courtesy of Raymond D. Parks; p. 8, Donald Miralle/Allsport; p. 27, Bill Hall/Allsport; p. 29, courtesy of Indianapolis Motor Speedway; p. 37, David Taylor/Allsport; pg. 48. Jamie Squire/Allsport

Text copyright © 2001 by Andrew Gutelle. Illustrations copyright © 2001 by Joel Snyder. All rights reserved. Published by Grosset & Dunlap, a division of Penguin Putnam Books for Young Readers, New York. GROSSET & DUNLAP and ALL ABOARD READING are trademarks of Penguin Putnam Inc. Published simultaneously in Canada. Printed in the U.S.A.

Library of Congress Cataloging-in-Publication Data is available.

ISBN 0-448-42489-4 (pbk)   A B C D E F G H I J
ISBN 0-448-42586-6 (GB)   A B C D E F G H I J

STOCK CAR
KINGS

By Andrew Gutelle
Illustrations by Joel Snyder

Grosset & Dunlap • New York

Introduction

February 15, 1948. Daytona Beach, Florida. Thousands of people crowd the beach. They will not swim, build sandcastles, or collect seashells. They are here to watch a race.

This is the first-ever contest run by the National Association for Stock Car Auto Racing. (It is called NASCAR, for short.) It is a race for stock cars only. Drivers in fancy racecars need not apply!

Fifty-six drivers gather on the sands at Daytona Beach. They turn on their car engines. The flagman waves a green flag. Go!

Cars rush over hard-packed sand. They race between the water and dunes. At the end of the beach, they make a sharp turn. Then they zoom back up the shore road.

Back and forth they go. Some cars get stuck in soft sand. Others crash and roll into the dunes. The tide is starting to come in. Will they finish the race in time?

After sixty-eight laps, Red Byron's Ford crosses the finish line. He has won NASCAR's first race!

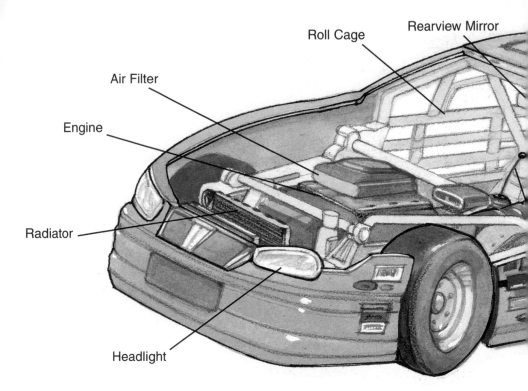

Roll Cage

Rearview Mirror

Air Filter

Engine

Radiator

Headlight

Today, stock car racing is more popular than ever. Huge speedways have replaced many beach and dirt tracks. Cars that roar around these roadways are painted with colorful designs. Each car is run by a racing team. A team works long hours trying to make its car the best.

A stock car is built from factory-made auto parts. In many ways, it is the same as an ordinary car. But there are differences, too. A stock car may have a more

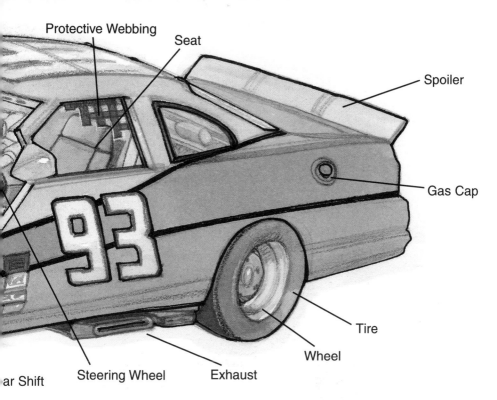

Protective Webbing
Seat
Spoiler
Gas Cap
Tire
Wheel
ar Shift
Steering Wheel
Exhaust

powerful engine. And some car parts, like the passenger seats, are removed from a stock car. Extra weight slows a car down. Drivers want their cars to go as fast as the rules will allow.

In a typical race, a driver circles a track 200 times or more. Each lap is a thrill-packed adventure. It is risky, too. Crashes are common. Thankfully, stock cars are built for safety as well as for speed. Even so, the danger remains. Some drivers have had their careers ended by serious accidents. A few, such as racing legend Dale Earnhardt, have even died in crashes.

The fans care a lot about their favorite drivers. Racing is a team sport. But the drivers take the greatest risk. They must go all out, all the time. Here are the stories of four champion drivers who have taken the challenge and won!

The King

July 4, 1984. Daytona International Speedway. Fans pack the grandstand. They sit in the hot Florida sun waiting for the start of the Pepsi Firecracker 400.

The racecars are on the track. People cheer as they spot the number 43 car. Richard Petty sits inside his blue Pontiac waiting for the race to begin. Petty is a fan favorite. They call him "The King."

King Richard has spent his life around racecars. Petty's father is a stock car legend. Lee Petty won the very first Daytona 500 in 1959. As a boy, Richard helped his father. He took apart engines and rebuilt them. Richard even worked as a one-kid pit crew for his father. At the time, he was only twelve years old!

Richard followed his dad into racing. That was twenty-six years ago. Since then, he has become the greatest stock car driver—ever! Richard has won 199 races in his career, nearly twice as many as any other driver. Is today the day he will reach the magic number of 200?

Win or lose, today's race will be special. Air Force One is flying to Daytona Beach. Ronald Reagan is on board. He wants be the first president to attend an auto race.

Over their headsets, the drivers hear a familiar voice. President Reagan says, "Gentleman, start your engines." The president is calling from his airplane. Let the race begin!

Petty starts the Firecracker 400 in sixth place. Another great driver, Cale

Yarborough, starts in first place, which is called the <u>pole position</u>. Yarborough starts first because he ran the fastest lap during the qualifying rounds that led up to the race. It gives him a slight edge at the start. And it tells drivers and fans that his car may be the fastest one on the track today.

Petty's car is fast, too. And he has loads of Daytona driving experience. He has won the Daytona 500 seven times. He knows how to get the most out of his car on this 2.5-mile track.

When the race begins, Richard quickly moves up toward the front of the pack. As the laps pile up, Petty and Yarborough leave the other cars behind. With twenty laps to go, they are a mile ahead of everyone else. One of these champions is sure to win. But which one?

With two laps to go, there is a minor accident. For the safety of all drivers, the car parts must be removed from the track.

The flagman waves the yellow flag. This is one of several flags used to send signals to the drivers. Just like a traffic light, green means "go," red means "stop," and yellow means "caution."

While the yellow flag is out, drivers may not pass other cars. But drivers <u>can</u>

pass until they reach the flag. With so few laps left, there will be no time to return to green. So the leader now is certain to win the race.

Petty hears his crew chief on his headset. "The caution flag is out. Take the lead. Now!"

Yarborough also knows the end of the race is near. He zooms forward in his Chevy. The next minute will decide who will win.

At first, Petty has the lead with Yarborough right on his bumper. Richard's

Pontiac wobbles a bit. Cale swings outside. He passes Petty and takes over first place!

Petty moves fast. He slides his car to the left. He wants to squeeze past on the inside part of the track. It is a risky move. If Yarborough gets there first, there will be no room to pass. The cars touch. They bump again and again. On the last bump, Petty squirts ahead. As they pass the yellow flag, he is in front!

After one more lap, the flagman takes down the yellow flag. He waves the black and white checkered flag. The race is over. Petty has won!

Petty races for eight more years. He thrills fans again and again. But the Firecracker 400 is Richard's final victory. Two hundred wins! It is a record that may last forever.

Awesome Bill

September 1, 1985. Darlington Raceway. South Carolina's famous old track is the site of an important event. One driver, Georgia's Bill Elliot, has a chance to win a million dollars!

This year, NASCAR has added a bonus award. It is called the Winston Million.

Any driver who competes in the Winston
Cup series of races can win the prize. But
it won't be easy. To collect it, a driver
must finish first in three of the four
biggest races of the year—the Daytona
500, the Winston 500, the World 600,
and the Southern 500.

No one dreamed a driver would quickly claim the prize. But if Elliot wins today's Southern 500, the bonus is his.

The Southern 500 race takes place on Labor Day weekend. Top stock car drivers have been competing week after week. They have raced about twenty-five times since their season began in February. For seven months, they have battled breakdowns, accidents, bad luck, and one another. Through it all, Bill Elliot has won. "Awesome Bill from Dawsonville" is having one of the greatest racing seasons ever!

Bill started fast. In February, his number 9 car won the Daytona 500 by nearly a mile. Three months later, he captured the Winston 500 at Talladega Superspeedway. Bill's car averaged 186.288 miles per hour. That was the fastest 500 miles in stock car history!

The Elliot brothers lead one of the

hottest teams in racing. Ernie Elliot is the crew chief. He and brother Dan also build the engines. Bill works on the body, or chassis, of the car. That helps when he is racing. He knows exactly how his car will handle on any part of the track.

By now, fans and drivers know Team Elliot's Ford Thunderbird is the best. But the fastest car does not always win. At the third big race of the year, the World

600 at the Charlotte Motor Speedway, Bill had car troubles. That day, he finished twenty-one laps behind the winner.

The Southern 500 is Elliot's last chance for the prize. Winning won't be easy. Darlington is much smaller than the superspeedways like Daytona. So Bill's speed edge won't help as much here. Also this old, egg-shaped track has sharp turns. Drivers must swing close to the outside walls. They often scrape against them. No wonder Darlington is called "The Track too Tough to Tame!"

At Darlington, it takes 367 laps to complete a 500-mile race. Since forty-three cars start each NASCAR race, drivers here have cars all around them! Elliott will need more than speed and skill to win today. He will need luck, too.

As he often has this year, Bill starts in the pole position. But early in the race, a problem pops up. His car does not feel right. Bill stays on the track as long as he can. When a yellow caution flag goes out, he heads for the pits. Ernie and the crew are waiting. A tire is badly damaged. One more lap and it might have blown! The crew changes the tire. Seconds later, Bill is back on the track.

Elliot works his car toward the front. He settles in as one of the leaders. If he can stay away from trouble, he has a good chance to win. Then, with less than seventy miles to go, he gets his next surprise.

On lap 319, Dale Earnhardt's car slips sideways in the track's second turn. Dale's car brushes the wall and slides across the track, right in front of Elliot. Bill steers his T-bird to the inside lane of the track. As Earnhardt goes by, the cars miss hitting each other by inches. How close was it? Bill doesn't know. "My eyes were shut," he says later.

Bill is not finished yet. On lap 324, another problem occurs. Cale Yarborough is leading, with Elliot close behind. Suddenly Cale's car spits out a

stream of smoke. Bill can't see! Again he swings toward the inside. He passes the smoking car just in time.

Elliot has the lead. But after a quick pit stop, Yarborough is back in the race. His T-bird is riding rough, but fast. With forty laps to go, he might catch up.

Bill drives carefully. He wants to stay away from trouble. But is he driving fast enough to win? With each mile, Yarborough gets closer. By the last lap, he is on Bill's tail. Skill and luck have carried Elliot this far. Now he uses a burst of speed to do the rest. Elliot's Thunderbird blazes across the finish line. He wins by .6 seconds!

Elliot has done it—barely. "This is the toughest race I've ever run," he says. "I thought it was never going to end."

Awesome Bill is thrilled. So are his fans. They give him a brand new nickname— "Million Dollar Bill."

Wonder Boy

August 6, 1994. Indianapolis Motor Speedway. This is America's oldest racetrack. For years, special racecars, Indy Cars, have run here. They have competed in the Indianapolis 500—the most famous auto race in America.

Today is a new day. Stock cars have come to Indy. A new race has been created just for them. It is called the Brickyard 400. (Brickyard is the track's nickname. Long ago, its racing surface was paved with bricks.)

For stock car fans, this is a special moment. There are 350,000 of them here. They want to see how their favorite drivers will handle this famous track.

The drivers are eager for the chance. And none of them is more excited than Jeff Gordon. Jeff's hometown is Pittsboro, Indiana. It is twenty miles away. For Jeff, racing at Indy is a dream come true.

Jeff is the youngest driver on the Winston Cup tour. He is called "Wonder Boy" or "The Kid." Although he is young, he has years of experience.

Jeff's stepfather bought him a mini-car when he was four years old. Jeff practiced and practiced. Soon he started racing his car. By the age of six, he was winning races. By seven, he was setting track records. As Jeff got older, he raced bigger cars. And he took on drivers much older than himself. By the time he graduated from high school, he had won 600 races. But that was racing for fun, as an amateur. Now Jeff had to prove he could beat the best professional drivers in the world.

Jeff Gordon drives the number 24 Chevy Lumina. It is painted with a colorful rainbow design. The men of his

pit crew are called the Rainbow Warriors.
They are led by crew chief Ray Evernham.

Ray is one of the best. During a race,
he talks to Jeff on his headset. Like all great
crew chiefs, his decisions in the pits can win
races.

In May, Jeff won the Coca-Cola 600. Ray
and the Rainbow Warriors were a big part

of that victory. On the last pit stop, Ray changed two tires instead of four. This quicker change saved several seconds and gave Jeff the lead. Jeff had to handle a rougher ride with two new tires and two old ones. Ray believed he could do it. He was right. That was Jeff's first win of the year. Would the Brickyard 400 be his second?

Most racers are driving at the Brickyard for the first time. That helps a driver like Jeff. He knows as much about the track

as anyone. Also, his quick reflexes and driving skill are perfect for Indy's sharp turns.

Jeff recorded the third fastest run in the time trials. So he starts in third place. As the race begins, Jeff stays near the front of the pack. He waits patiently for a chance to take charge.

Geoff Bodine's Ford Thunderbird seems to be the fastest car today. But luck is against him. On lap 101, his brother Brett bumps his car. Geoff spins right out of the race.

Gordon is ready. He surges to the front, but he is not alone. Jeff sees another driver in his rearview mirror. Here comes "Swervin" Ernie Irvan! Ernie is one of the toughest drivers on the track. "The last person I wanted to race at the end was Ernie," says Gordon.

Jeff and Ernie battle for twenty laps. At times they are bumper-to-bumper. Often they drive side-by-side. They are so close, their wheels nearly touch!

The pace is intense. The cars start wearing down. Something has to give. With four laps to go, Irvan's tire blows out. He heads for the pit.

Gordon has the lead. He blazes through four more laps. Then he takes the checkered flag. The winner!

On his victory lap, Jeff is so happy he nearly cries. "Oh my God. I did it! I did it!" he shouts to Evernham over his headset.

Jeff has reached the top. The Brickyard 400 is his second victory. Since that day, his win total has passed fifty. He is still young and he is one of the best. With "The Kid" behind the wheel, the future of the colorful number 24 car looks very bright.

The Intimidator

February 15, 1998. Daytona
International Speedway. Fifty years ago,
Red Byron won on the sands of Daytona
Beach. Today, stock car fans gather at the
city's superspeedway. A new racing season
is about to begin. As always, it begins with
the Daytona 500.

This is the twentieth Daytona 500 for
Dale Earnhardt. He has won other races
here, but never the 500. In the past, Dale
has come close, amazingly close:

- 1986: Dale leads but runs out of gas with a few laps to go.
- 1990: In front after 499 miles, Dale's car gets a flat tire on the last lap.
- 1993: Earnhardt loses a last lap duel to Dale Jarrett by .12 of a second.
- 1996: Jarrett beats Earnhardt by .17 of a second.

Dale attacks the track in his black Monte Carlo. He drives hard and close. No wonder he is called "The Intimidator." His fans are here today hoping to see his aggressive driving style.

Dale comes to Daytona on the worst losing streak of his career. He has lost fifty-nine races in a row. It has been nearly two years since he won a race. Even his fans wonder: Is the forty-six-year-old driver too old? Will he ever win again?

If Dale is going to win, he will have to beat Jeff Gordon. "The Kid" is the defending champ and the previous season's Driver of the Year. He is the man to beat.

Dale starts the race in fourth place. As usual, he drives all out. By lap seventeen, he is in the lead. But there is a long way to go in this 200-lap race.

Gordon starts all the way back in twenty-ninth place. He zips past one car after another. After a quick pit stop, he takes over first place on lap fifty-nine.

Gordon is fast today, but he is not lucky. On lap 123, his car hits some debris. The damage does not wreck his car. But it makes number 24 harder to handle. Jeff's chances of winning are slim.

Earnhardt is riding second. He zooms past Gordon and into the lead. But there are nearly 200 miles to go. And behind him there are two drivers coming on fast!

Jeremy Mayfield and Rusty Wallace are part of the same racing team. Although each wants to win, they can do things as teammates that help them both.

Mayfield and Wallace drive single file. The air flows over their cars together and boosts their speed. This racing trick is called drafting. Since Earnhardt is alone, he cannot draft. It is only a matter of time until the two cars pass him.

Dale needs a little luck. On lap 173 he gets a break. Because of a minor accident on another part of the track, officials fly the yellow caution flag. Mayfield and Wallace must wait to pass.

The yellow flag gives Earnhardt a chance to make a fast pit stop. He gets two new tires and just enough gas to finish the race. This quick stop lets him keep the lead. But will Mayfield and Wallace catch up anyway?

Dale looks in his rearview mirror. He sees Mike Skinner charging toward him. Mike is Dale's teammate. He drafts behind Dale. This gives Earnhardt the speed boost he needs!

Dale hangs on. When the caution goes out once again near the end of the race, it is all over. Dale cruises to victory. The Daytona 500! Finally!

The race is over, but not the celebration. Dale takes a victory lap. In the stands, 175,000 fans—the largest Daytona crowd in history—cheer. On the track, all the pit crews come out. They line Pit Road, which runs along the front stretch of track. As Dale rolls slowly by, they applaud. Many shake his hand through the open window of his number 3 car.

Next Earnhardt drives onto the track infield. He wants to celebrate. Turning sharply, his wheels cut several circles, called donuts, in the grass. Then he drives onto Victory Lane. At last, he is in the winner's circle. He says happily, "It was my time."

Author's Note

February 18, 2001, was a sad day for stock car racing fans everywhere. Dale Earnhardt died in a car crash. He was 49 years old.

The accident took place during the Daytona 500. Dale was near the end of the race. At the time, he was in third place. His teammate, Michael Waltrip, and his son, Dale Jr., were the only drivers in front of him.

Auto racing is exciting. Sadly, it is dangerous, too. That is why racing teams do all they can to make sure drivers are safe. For example, every stock car has a steel cage built into it. If the car rolls over in a crash, the steel protects the driver.

New safety devices are being added all the time. Some drivers now wear a HANS device. (The name stands for *Head and Neck Support*.) It attaches to a driver's helmet. A HANS device provides greater protection in crashes.

Another new safety measure is appearing on some tracks. The concrete walls are padded with foam barriers. These soften the blow when a car hits a wall. Would a HANS device or foam barrier have saved Dale Earnhardt? No one knows for sure.

Dale was a racing legend. He will be remembered for his hard-driving style and his many victories. Hopefully his death will change his sport. Officials, car owners, and racing teams will try even harder to protect drivers. Everyone will work to make stock car racing as safe as it can be. If that happens, Dale will be remembered for that, too.

Dale Earnhardt
1951-2001